MEXICAN COOKING

TIGER BOOKS INTERNATIONAL
LONDON

2063
This 1993 edition published by Tiger Books International PLC, London
© 1989 Coombe Books
ISBN 1-85501-227-8

INTRODUCTION

In Mexico, as in most countries of the world that enjoy warm climates, the food is spicy. The addition of spices to food cooked in these climates has a two-fold purpose: they act as a preservative while also stimulating appetites flagging in the heat. But just because food is spicy, it need not be very hot. Cumin, coriander and cinnamon are favourite choices in Mexico and lend their fragrance and flavour without bringing tears to the eyes! For those who like things hot, fresh or dried chilli peppers or cayenne pepper will add fire to any dish. Green chillies and Jalapeno peppers, another variety, are also available canned.

If any one ingredient really symbolises Mexican cooking, it is the tortilla. In Mexico, tortillas in one form or another appear at every meal. Even if they are not an integral part of a recipe they are served warm as an accompaniment, even with eggs at breakfast. There are two types of tortilla, each made with different flours. Corn tortillas are made with Masa Harina, a fine corn flour that is not always easy to find. These corn tortillas are also slightly more difficult to make and to work with even though they are the more popular choice in Mexico. However, in the northern part of the country more wheat is grown, so tortillas are more often made with wheat flour. These are easy to make and more pliable, so they are easier to use in recipes and many people prefer them to the corn variety. Our recipe for flour tortillas can be used interchangeably with corn tortillas and you can even cut the tortillas into triangles or rounds and deep-fry them to make your own tortilla chips.

The use of cocoa powder in savoury dishes may seem a startling idea, but don't be put off. It gives a depth of colour and flavour to meat dishes without making them taste of chocolate. Spanish settlers in Mexico first used the plentiful cocoa bean in their cooking, adapting it to both sweet and savoury dishes. While the Spanish also introduced sugar and milk into the cuisine, sweets have not become overly popular in Mexico.

Over the past few years more and more prepared ingredients for Mexican cooking have appeared on the market. Corn tortillas come ready made and even shaped exactly right for tacos, making the cook's job easy. But, there is fun to be had in cooking this colourful and exciting cuisine in the traditional way, too.

MAKES ½ PINT

Taco Sauce

This basic recipe has many uses in Mexican cooking – sauce, topping, dip or as an ingredient to give a dish extra flavour.

15ml/1 tbsp oil
1 onion, diced
1 green pepper, diced
½-1 red or green chilli pepper
2.5ml/½ tsp ground cumin
2.5ml/½ tsp ground coriander
½ clove garlic, crushed
Pinch salt, pepper and sugar
400g/14oz canned tomatoes
Tomato purée (optional)

Step 3 Add remaining ingredients and use a potato masher or fork to break up tomatoes.

Step 2 Cut the chilli in half, remove the seeds and chop flesh finely.

Step 4 Cook the sauce over moderate heat to reduce and thicken.

1. Heat the oil in a heavy-based saucepan and when hot, add the onion and pepper. Cook slowly to soften slightly.

2. Chop the chilli and add with the cumin, coriander, garlic and cook a further 2-3 minutes.

3. Add sugar, seasonings and tomatoes with their juice.

Break up the tomatoes with a fork or a potato masher.

4. Cook a further 5-6 minutes over moderate heat to reduce and thicken slighly. Add tomato purée for colour, if necessary. Adjust seasoning and use hot or cold according to your recipe.

Cook's Notes

Time
Preparation takes about 15-20 minutes, cooking takes about 8-10 minutes.

Serving Ideas
Use as a sauce or topping for fish, meat or poultry main dishes. Use in tacos, tostadas, nachos and as a dip for tortilla chips or vegetable crudites

Freezing
Fill rigid containers with sauce at room temperature. Label and freeze for up to 3 months. Defrost at room temperature, breaking the sauce up as it thaws.

MAKES 12

FLOUR TORTILLAS

Tortillas made with wheat instead of corn are
traditional in Northern Mexico. Flour tortillas
are easier to make and use than the corn variety.

450g/1lb plain or wholemeal flour
15g/1 tbsp salt
90g/6 tbsps lard
280ml/½ pint hot water

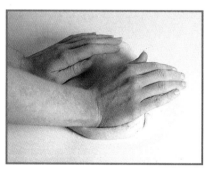

Step 2 Knead a ball of prepared dough until smooth and pliable.

1. Sift flour and salt into a mixing bowl and rub in the lard until the mixture resembles fine breadcrumbs. Mix in the water gradually to form a soft, pliable dough. Wholemeal flour may need more water.

2. Knead on a well-floured surface until smooth and no longer sticky. Cover with a damp tea towel.

3. Cut off about 45g/3 tbsps of dough at a time, keeping the rest covered. Knead into a ball.

4. Roll the ball of dough out into a very thin circle with a floured rolling pin. Cut into a neat round using a 25cm/10 inch plate as a guide. Continue until all the dough is used.

5. Stack the tortillas as you make them, flouring each well to prevent sticking. Cover with a clean tea towel.

6. Heat a heavy-based frying pan and carefully place in a tortilla. Cook for about 10 seconds per side. Stack and keep covered until all are cooked. Use according to chosen recipe.

Step 4 Roll out the ball of dough thinly and cut into a 25cm/10 inch circle.

Step 6 Cook for 10 seconds per side in a hot frying pan.

Cook's Notes

Time
Preparation takes about 60 minutes to make the dough and roll out all the tortillas, cooking takes about 5 minutes.

Serving Ideas
Use with any recipe that calls for tortillas. Also, serve hot as an accompaniment to any Mexican dish.

Freezing
Tortillas can be prepared and cooked in advance and frozen. Stack the tortillas between sheets of non-stick or wax paper. Place in plastic bags, seal, label and freeze for up to 2 months. Defrost at room temperature before using.

SERVES 8

GUACAMOLE

This is one of Mexico's most famous dishes.
It is delicious as a first course on its
own or as an ingredient in other recipes.

1 medium onion, finely chopped
1 clove garlic, crushed
Grated rind and juice of ½ lime
½ quantity Taco Sauce recipe
3 large avocados
15ml/1 tbsp chopped fresh coriander
Pinch salt
Coriander leaves to garnish
1 package tortilla chips

Step 3 Hit the stone with a large knife and twist to remove the stone.

Step 2 Cut avocados in half and twist the halves to separate.

Step 6 Use a potato masher to mash the avocado until nearly smooth.

1. Mix the onion, garlic, rind and juice of lime and the taco sauce together in a large mixing bowl.

2. Cut the avocados in half lengthways. Twist the halves gently in opposite directions to separate.

3. Hit the stone with a large, sharp knife and twist the knife to remove the stone.

4. Place the avocado halves cut side down on a chopping board. Lightly score the skin lengthwise and gently pull back to peel. Alternatively, scoop out avocado flesh with a spoon, scraping the skin well.

5. Chop the avocado roughly and immediately place in the bowl with the onion and lime.

6. Use a potato masher to break up the avocado until almost smooth. Do not over-mash. Season with salt and stir in the chopped coriander. Spoon into a serving bowl and garnish with coriander leaves.

7. Surround the bowl with tortilla chips for dipping.

Cook's Notes

Time
Preparation takes about 25 minutes.

Preparation
Do not prepare too long in advance. The avocado will darken even with the addition of lime juice if left too long.

Cook's Tip
Try leaving the avocado stone in the mixture. This is said to retard discolouration.

SERVES 4

MOYETTES

While these sandwiches seem like lunch fare, they
are very popular for breakfast in Mexico.

4 crusty rolls
30g/2 tbsps butter or margarine
225g/8oz canned refried beans
2 spring onions, chopped
60g/4 tbsps grated Tilsit cheese

1. Cut the rolls in half and remove some of the inside.

Step 2 Spread both sides of each roll with softened butter or margarine, then fill the rolls with the refried beans.

Step 1 Remove some of the insides of each roll. Use a teaspoon to scrape out crumbs or cut out with a small knife.

2. Soften the butter and spread on both sides of the rolls.

3. Fill the rolls with the refried beans.

4. Sprinkle with the onion and top with the grated cheese.

5. Place the rolls on a baking sheet and cook in a preheated 160°C/325°F/Gas Mark 3 oven for 15-20 minutes, or until the cheese has melted and the beans are hot. Serve immediately.

Cook's Notes

Time
Preparation takes about 15 minutes and cooking takes about 15-20 minutes.

Cook's Tip
Sandwiches may be prepared in advance and heated through just before serving. Once heated, they do not reheat successfully.

Variation
Use red onion and Cheddar or Monterey Jack cheese, if available.

MAKES 12

TACOS

Packaged taco shells make this famous
Mexican snack easy to prepare, so spend
the extra time on imaginative fillings.

12 taco shells

Beef Filling

15ml/1 tbsp oil
450g/1lb minced beef
1 medium onion, chopped
10ml/2 tsps ground cumin
1 clove garlic, crushed
10ml/2 tsps chilli powder
Pinch paprika
Salt and pepper

Chicken Filling

45g/3 tbsps butter or margarine
1 medium onion, chopped
1 small red pepper, seeded and chopped
30g/2 tbsps flaked almonds
340g/12oz chicken breasts, skinned and finely chopped
Salt and pepper
1 piece fresh ginger, peeled and chopped
90ml/6 tbsps milk
10ml/2 tsps cornflour
140ml/¼ pint sour cream

Toppings

Shredded lettuce
Grated cheese
Tomatoes, seeded and chopped
Chopped spring onions
Avocado slices
Sour cream
Jalapeno peppers
Taco sauce

1. Heat oil for beef filling in a large frying pan and brown the beef and onions, breaking the meat up with a fork as it cooks. Add spices, garlic and seasoning and cook about 20 minutes. Set aside.

2. Melt the 30g/2 tbsps butter or margarine in a medium saucepan and add the onion. Cook slowly until softened.

3. Add the red pepper and almonds and cook slowly until the almonds are lightly browned. Stir often during cooking. Remove to a plate and set aside.

4. Melt the remaining butter in the same saucepan and cook the chicken for about 5 minutes, turning frequently. Season and return the onion mixture to the pan along with the chopped ginger.

5. Blend milk and cornflour and stir into the chicken mixture. Bring to the boil and stir until very thick. Mix in the sour cream and cook gently to heat through. Do not boil.

6. Heat the taco shells on a baking sheet in a preheated 180°C/350°F/Gas Mark 4 oven for 2-3 minutes. Place on the sheet with the open ends down.

7. To fill, hold the shell in one hand and spoon in about 15ml/1 tbsp of either beef or chicken filling.

8. Next, add a layer of shredded lettuce, followed by a layer of grated cheese.

9. Add choice of other toppings and finally spoon on some taco sauce.

Step 7 Hold taco shell in the palm of the hand and fill with about 15ml/1 tbsp filling.

Cook's Notes

 Time
Preparation takes about 40 minutes. Cooking takes about 20 minutes for the beef filling, 15 minutes for the chicken filling and 2-3 minutes to heat the taco shells.

 Cook's Tip
Placing the taco shells on their open ends when reheating keeps them from closing up and makes filling easier.

Serving Ideas
For a buffet, place all the ingredients out separately for guests to help themselves and create their own combinations.

SERVES 8-10

NACHOS

These make excellent cocktail savouries
and the variety of toppings and flavour
combinations is almost endless.

1 package round tortilla chips
1 can refried beans
1 can Jalapeno bean dip
Full quantity Taco Sauce recipe
8-10 cherry tomatoes, sliced
140ml/¼ pint sour cream or natural yogurt
Sliced black and stuffed green olives
Grated Cheddar cheese

Taco Filling

10ml/2 tsps oil
225g/8oz minced beef
10ml/2 tsps chilli powder
Pinch ground coriander
Pinch cayenne pepper
Salt and pepper

1. Prepare taco filling as for Tacos recipe. Top half of the tortilla chips with refried beans and half with beef taco filling.

2. Place a spoonful of taco sauce on the bean-topped chips and Jalapeno bean dip in the beef-topped chips.

3. Top the tortilla chips with tomatoes, sour cream or yogurt, olives or cheese in any desired combination, and serve.

Step 2 Spoon on taco sauce and Jalapeno bean dip on top of beans or beef.

Step 1 Use a teaspoon to top chips with beans and beef mixture. Spread out carefully with the bowl of the spoon.

Step 3 Top with chosen ingredients and serve. Heat through to melt cheese if desired.

Cook's Notes

Time
Preparation takes about 25 minutes.

Variation
If desired, heat through for 5 minutes in a moderate oven before topping with tomatoes, sour cream or olives. Cheese may be sprinkled on to melt before serving.

Cook's Tip
Tortilla chips will become slightly soggy if topped too soon before serving.

MAKES 12

TOSTADAS

These are popular all over Mexico and the toppings reflect the food available in each area. They are delicious, but difficult to eat!

10ml/2 tsps oil
450g/1lb minced beef or pork
10ml/2 tsps chilli powder
5ml/1 tsp ground cumin
5ml/1 tsp ground coriander
1 can refried beans
1 package tostada shells

Toppings

Shredded lettuce
Grated Cheddar cheese
Tomatoes, seeded and chopped
Sour Cream
Olives
Prawns
Spring onions, chopped
Taco sauce

Step 4 Spoon some of the meat mixture over the beans, pushing it down gently so that it sticks to the beans.

Step 5 Top with your choice of topping ingredients.

Step 3 Spread refried beans carefully over each tostada shell.

1. Cook the meat in the oil in a medium frying pan. Sprinkle on the spices and cook quickly to brown.

2. Reheat the beans and place the tostada shells on a baking sheet. Heat 2-3 minutes in a moderate oven.

3. Spread 15-30ml/1-2 tbsps of the beans on each tostada shell.

4. Top each shell with some of the beef mixture.

5. Add the topping ingredients in different combinations and serve immediately.

Cook's Notes

Time
Preparation takes about 40 minutes, cooking takes about 10-15 minutes.

Preparation
All the ingredients can be prepared ahead of time. The tostadas cannot be reheated once assembled.

Variation
Add chopped green or red peppers to the list of toppings along with chopped green chillies or Jalapeno peppers and guacamole.

SERVES 6

FLAUTAS

Traditionally, these are long, thin
rolls of tortillas with savoury
fillings, topped with sour cream.

225g/8oz chicken, skinned, boned and minced or finely
   chopped
15ml/1 tbsp oil
1 small onion, finely chopped
½ green pepper, finely chopped
½-1 chilli pepper, seeded and finely chopped
90g/3oz frozen sweetcorn
6 black olives, pitted and chopped
120ml/4 fl oz double cream
Salt
12 prepared tortillas (see recipe for Flour Tortillas)
Taco sauce, guacamole and sour cream for toppings.

1. Use a food processor or meat mincer to prepare the
chicken, or chop by hand.

2. Heat the oil in a medium frying pan and add the
chicken, onion and green pepper. Cook over moderate
heat, stirring frequently to break up the pieces of chicken.

3. When the chicken is cooked and the vegetables are
softened, add the chilli, sweetcorn, olives, cream and salt.
Bring to the boil over heat and boil rapidly, stirring
continuously, to reduce and thicken the cream.

4. Place 2 tortillas on a clean work surface, overlapping
them by about 5cm/2 inches. Spoon some of the chicken
mixture onto the tortillas, roll up and secure with cocktail
sticks.

5. Fry the flautas in about 1.25cm/½ inch oil in a large
frying pan. Do not allow the tortillas to get very brown. Drain
on paper towels.

6. Arrange flautas on serving plates and top with sour
cream, guacamole and taco sauce.

Step 4 Place
tortillas slightly
overlapping on
work surface and
fill with chicken.

Step 4 Use
cocktail sticks to
secure tortillas.

Step 5 Fry slowly
and turn carefully
so the filling does
not leak.

Cook's Notes

Time
Preparation takes about 1
hour for the tortillas and about
30 minutes to finish the dish.

Variation
Use pork or beef in place of
the chicken. Green olives,
may be substituted for black, and red
peppers for green.

Serving Ideas
Flautas are often served with
rice, refried beans and a
salad.

SERVES 6

BURRITOS

The name means 'little donkeys' and the dish is
a very popular one. Beans are the traditional
filling, but meat may be used as well.

6 flour tortillas
1 onion, chopped
15ml/1 tbsp oil
450g/1lb canned refried beans
6 lettuce leaves, shredded
30ml/2 tbsps snipped chives
2 tomatoes, sliced
120g/4oz Cheddar cheese, grated
Full quantity Taco Sauce recipe
140ml/¼ pint sour cream
Chopped coriander leaves

Step 3 Use kitchen scissors to make snipping chives easy.

Step 3 Spoon some of the bean mixture down the centre of each tortilla.

Step 3 Fold the ends and sides of each tortilla around the filling to make rectangular parcels.

1. Wrap tortillas in foil and heat in a warm oven to soften.

2. Cook the onion in the oil until soft but not coloured. Add the beans and heat through.

3. Spoon the mixture down the centre of each tortilla. Top with lettuce, cheese, tomatoes and chives. Fold over the

sides to form long rectangular parcel. Make sure the filling is completely enclosed.

4. Place burritos in an ovenproof dish, cover and cook in a preheated 180°C/350°F/Gas Mark 4 oven for about 20 minutes.

5. Spoon over the taco sauce. Top with sour cream and sprinkle with chopped coriander to serve.

Cook's Notes

🕐 **Time**
Preparation takes about 25 minutes, not including making the tortillas. Cooking takes about 20 minutes.

📐 **Preparation**
Heat just before serving. Burritos do not reheat well. Add extra chilli pepper to the taco sauce recipe if desired.

 Serving Ideas
Serve with rice and guacamole.

SERVES 6

CHIMICHANGAS

A strange sounding name for a delicious snack
which is something like a deep-fried taco.

6 flour tortillas
Half quantity Chilli Con Carne recipe
6 lettuce leaves, shredded
6 spring onions, chopped
90g/3oz Cheddar cheese, grated
Oil for frying
Half quantity Guacamole recipe
140ml/¼ pint sour cream
1 tomato, seeded and chopped

Step 4 Lower the chimichangas carefully into hot oil in a large frying pan, folded side first.

Step 3 Fold the tortillas over the filling to enclose it completely and form a parcel.

Step 5 After about 3 minutes, turn chimichangas over with a draining spoon or fish slice to cook the other side.

1. Wrap the tortillas in foil and place in a warm oven for 5 minutes to make them pliable.

2. Heat the chilli briefly and spoon about 30ml/2 tbsps onto the centre of each tortilla. Top with lettuce, onions and cheese.

3. Fold in the sides to make a parcel, making sure all the filling is enclosed.

4. Heat about 2.5cm/1 inch of oil in a large frying pan and

when hot lower in the chimichangas, folded side down first. Cook 2-4 at a time depending on the size of the pan.

5. Cook for 3 minutes and carefully turn over. Cook a further 3 minutes and remove to paper towels and drain. Repeat with remaining chimichangas.

6. Spoon the guacamole over the top of each and drizzle over the sour cream. Sprinkle over the chopped tomato and serve immediately.

Cook's Notes

Time
Preparation takes about 30 minutes. This does not include time to prepare the tortillas or the chilli. Cooking time for the chimichangas is about 12-18 minutes.

Preparation
Tortillas and chilli can be made in advance and the chimichangas cooked just before serving. They do not reheat successfully.

Serving Idea
Serve with rice and refried beans.

SERVES 6

ENCHILADAS

Although fillings and sauces vary, enchiladas
are one of the tastiest Mexican dishes.

10 ripe tomatoes, peeled, seeded and chopped
1 small onion, chopped
1-2 green or red chillies, seeded and chopped
1 clove garlic, crushed
Salt
Pinch sugar
15-30ml/1-2 tbsps tomato purée
30g/2 tbsps butter or margarine
2 eggs
280ml/½ pint double cream
60g/4 tbsps grated cheese
340g/12oz minced pork
1 small red pepper, seeded and chopped
60g/4 tbsps raisins
60g/4 tbsps pine nuts
Salt and pepper
12 prepared tortillas (see recipe for Flour Tortillas)
Sliced spring onions to garnish

1. Place tomatoes, onion, chillies, garlic, salt and sugar in
a blender or food processor and purée until smooth.

2. Melt butter or margarine in a large saucepan. Add the
purée and simmer for 5 minutes.

3. Beat together the eggs and cream, mixing well. Add a
spoonful of the hot tomato purée to the cream and eggs
and mix quickly. Return mixture to the saucepan with the
rest of the tomato purée. Reserve cheese for topping.

4. Heat slowly, stirring constantly, until the mixture thick-
ens. Do not boil.

5. While preparing the sauce, cook the pork and pepper
slowly in a large frying pan. Use a fork to break up the meat
as it cooks. Turn up the heat when the pork is nearly cooked
and fry briskly for a few minutes. Add the raisins, pine nuts

and seasoning.

6. Combine about ¼ of the sauce with the meat and divide
mixture evenly among all the tortillas. Spoon on the filling to
one side of the centre and roll up the tortilla around it,
leaving the ends open and some of the filling showing.

7. Place enchiladas seam side down in a baking dish and
pour over the remaining sauce, leaving the ends uncover-
ed. Sprinkle over the cheese and bake in a preheated
180°C/350°F/Gas Mark 4 oven for 15-20 minutes, or until
the sauce begins to bubble. Sprinkle with the sliced onions
and serve immediately.

Step 3 Mix the eggs and cream with some of the hot sauce and then return it to the pan, stirring constantly.

Step 6 Spoon meat filling to one side of the tortillas and roll them up, leaving ends open.

Cook's Notes

 Time
Preparation takes about 60
minutes to make the tortillas
and about 30 minutes more to finish the
dish.

Watchpoint
When preparing the sauce, do
not allow it to boil or it
will curdle.

Economy
Left-over meat or chicken can
be minced in a food processor
or finely chopped and used in place of
the freshly cooked meat.

SERVES 4

PRAWNS ACAPULCO

These make a stylish starter or a quickly
prepared snack. Make the bread slices
smaller to serve with cocktails.

4 slices bread, crusts removed
90g/6 tbsps softened butter
180g/6oz cooked and peeled prawns
2.5ml/½ tsp chilli powder
1.25ml/¼ tsp paprika
1.25ml/¼ tsp cumin
Salt and pepper
Watercress to garnish

1. Cut the bread slices in half and spread with 30g/2 tbsps butter. Butter both sides sparingly.

2. Place the bread on a baking sheet and cook in a preheated 180°C/350°F/Gas Mark 4 oven for 10-15 minutes until golden brown. Keep warm.

3. Melt the remaining butter in a small pan and add the prawns, spices and seasoning and stir well.

4. Heat through completely and spoon on top of the bread slices. Garnish with watercress and serve hot.

Step 2 Cook the bread on a baking sheet until golden brown and crisp.

Step 3 Cook the prawn and chilli mixture over gentle heat, stirring continuously.

Cook's Notes

Time
Preparation takes about 15 minutes. The bread will take 15-20 minutes to cook until golden, and the prawns take about 5 minutes to heat through.

Watchpoint
Do not heat the prawns too long or at too high a temperature; they toughen easily.

Cook's Tip
The bread may be prepared in advance and reheated 5 minutes in the oven. Do not reheat the prawns.

SERVES 4

CHILLI VEGETABLE SOUP

A simple-to-make and delicious soup
that makes a light first course.

15ml/1 tbsp oil
1 onion, chopped
120g/4oz canned whole green chillies, quartered
1 litre/2 pints chicken stock
1 large potato, peeled and cut into short strips
Full quantity Taco Sauce recipe
15ml/1 tbsp lime juice
Tortilla chips and lime slices to garnish
Salt

1. Heat the oil in a large saucepan and sauté the onion until translucent. Add the green chillies, stock, potato and taco sauce.

2. Cover the pan and simmer soup for 20 minutes. Stir in the lime juice and add salt.

3. Serve in individual bowls with tortilla chips.

4. Cut a thin slice of lime to float in each bowl of soup.

Step 1 Cook the onion slowly in the oil until translucent. Do not brown.

Step 1 Add the remaining ingredients and simmer for 20 minutes.

Cook's Notes

Time
Preparation takes about 20 minutes and cooking takes 20 minutes.

Variation
Use only half a can green chillies if desired, or cook green peppers with the onions instead.

Serving Ideas
For a more filling soup, add cooked rice.

SERVES 4
BEEF & BEAN SOUP

In Mexico, the day's main meal is
eaten at around 2.00 pm and this
soup is a popular starter.

1 large onion, peeled and finely chopped
2 sticks celery, chopped
1 red pepper, deseeded and finely chopped
30ml/2 tbsps oil
225g/8oz minced beef
6 tomatoes, peeled, seeded and chopped
420g/15oz canned refried beans
5ml/1 tsp ground cumin
5ml/1 tsp chilli powder
5ml/1 tsp garlic powder or purée
Pinch cinnamon and cayenne pepper
570ml/1 pint beef stock
Salt and pepper

Step 1 Cook the onion, celery and pepper in oil to soften. Stir frequently.

1. Fry the onion, pepper and celery in the oil in a large saucepan until softened.

2. Add the beef and fry over medium heat until well browned. Add the tomatoes and refried beans with the spices, garlic and seasoning and mix well.

3. Stir in the stock and bring to the boil. Cover and simmer gently for 30 minutes, stirring occasionally.

4. Pour the soup into a blender or food processor and purée. The soup will be quite thick and not completely smooth.

5. Adjust the seasoning and serve with tortilla chips. Top with sour cream if desired.

Step 2 Cook the beef over medium heat until well browned.

Step 4 Purée the soup in several batches until nearly smooth.

Cook's Notes

Time
Preparation takes about 20 minutes and cooking takes about 50 minutes to soften vegetables, brown meat and simmer soup.

Watchpoint
Make sure the blender or food processor lid is closed securely before puréeing the hot soup. Purée in 2 or 3 small batches for safety.

Freezing
Allow the puréed soup to cool completely and skim any fat from the surface. Pour into freezer containers, label and freeze for up to 3 months.

SERVES 6

Mexican Chicken & Pepper Salad

This is the perfect lunch or light supper dish
during the summer, and it can be prepared in advance.

450g/1lb cooked chicken, cut in strips
140ml/¼ pint mayonnaise
140ml/¼ pint natural yogurt
5ml/1 tsp chilli powder
5ml/1 tsp paprika
Pinch cayenne pepper
2.5ml/½ tsp tomato purée
5ml/1 tsp onion purée
1 green pepper, seeded and finely sliced
1 red pepper, seeded and finely sliced
180g/6oz frozen sweetcorn, defrosted
180g/6oz long grain rice, cooked

1. Place the chicken strips in a large salad bowl.

2. Mix the mayonnaise, yogurt, spices, tomato and onion purées together and leave to stand briefly for flavours to blend. Fold dressing into the chicken.

3. Add the peppers and sweetcorn and mix gently until all the ingredients are coated with dressing.

4. Place the rice on a serving dish and pile the salad into the centre. Serve immediately.

Step 3 Fold all ingredients together gently so that they do not break up. Use a large spoon or rubber spatula.

Step 4 Arrange rice on a serving plate and spoon salad into the centre.

Cook's Notes

Time
Preparation takes about 30 minutes.

Buying Guide
Onion purée is available in tubes like tomato purée.

Preparation
Chicken salad may be prepared several hours in advance and kept covered in the refrigerator. Spoon onto rice just before serving.

Variation
Add sliced or diced green chillies or Jalapeno peppers for hotter flavour. Try chilli sauce or taco sauce as an alternative seasoning.

SERVES 6

CHILLI PRAWN QUICHE

Fresh chilli peppers give a Mexican flavour
to this quiche with its prawn filling.

Pastry

120g/4oz plain flour
Pinch salt
30g/2 tbsps butter or margarine
30g/2 tbsps white cooking fat
30-60ml/2-4 tbsps cold water

Filling

4 eggs
140ml/¼ pint milk
140ml/¼ pint single cream
½ clove garlic, crushed
120g/4oz Cheddar cheese, grated
3 spring onions, chopped
2 green chillies, seeded and chopped
225g/8oz cooked and peeled prawns
Salt
Cooked, unpeeled prawns and parsley sprigs for garnish

1. Sift the flour with a pinch of salt into a mixing bowl, or place in a food processor and mix once or twice.

2. Rub in the butter and fat until the mixture resembles fine breadcrumbs, or work in the food processor, being careful not to over-mix.

3. Mix in the liquid gradually, adding enough to bring the pastry together into a ball. In a food processor, add the liquid through the funnel while the machine is running.

4. Wrap the pastry well and chill for 20-30 minutes.

5. Roll out the pastry on a well-floured surface with a floured rolling pin.

6. Wrap the circle of pastry around the rolling pin to lift it into a 25cm/10 inch flan dish. Unroll the pastry over the dish.

7. Carefully press the pastry onto the bottom and up the sides of the dish, taking care not to stretch it.

8. Roll the rolling pin over the top of the dish to remove excess pastry, or cut off with a sharp knife.

9. Mix the eggs, milk, cream and garlic together. Sprinkle the cheese, onion, chillies and prawns onto the base of the pastry and pour over the egg mixture.

10. Bake in a preheated 200°C/400°F/Gas Mark 6 oven for 30-40 minutes until firm and golden brown. Peel the tail shells off the prawns and remove the legs and roe if present. Use to garnish the quiche along with the sprigs of parsley.

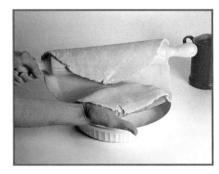

Step 6 Use the rolling pin to help lift the pastry into the flan dish.

Step 7 Carefully press the pastry into the dish to line the base and sides.

Cook's Notes

Time
Preparation takes about 40 minutes, which includes time for the pastry to chill. Cooking takes 30-40 minutes.

Variation
Add diced red or green peppers and chopped coriander leaves to the filling before baking.

Serving Ideas
Serve as a starter, cut in thin wedges or baked in individual dishes. Serve hot or cold with a salad for a snack or light meal.

SERVES 6

PRAWNS VERACRUZ

Veracruz is a port on the Gulf of Mexico
which lends its name to a variety
of colourful seafood dishes.

15ml/1 tbsp oil
1 onion, chopped
1 large green pepper, cut into 3.5cm/1½ inch strips.
2-3 green chillies, seeded and chopped
Double quantity Taco Sauce recipe
2 tomatoes, skinned and roughly chopped
12 pimento-stuffed olives, halved
10ml/2 tsps capers
1.25ml/¼ tsp ground cumin
Salt
450g/1lb prawns, uncooked
Juice of 1 lime

Refresh in cold water. The skins will now peel away easily.

Place the tomatoes in a pan of boiling water for a few seconds.

Step 2 Combine all the sauce ingredients in a heavy-based pan.

cumin and salt. Bring to the boil and then lower the heat to simmer for 5 minutes.

1. Heat the oil in a large frying pan and add the onion and green pepper. Cook until soft but not coloured.

2. Add chillies, taco sauce, tomatoes, olives, capers,

3. Remove black veins, if present, from the rounded side of the prawns with a cocktail stick.

4. Add the prawns to the sauce and cook until they curl up and turn pink and opaque. Add the lime juice to taste and serve.

Cook's Notes

Time
Preparation takes about 25 minutes and cooking takes about 15 minutes.

Preparation
Sauce may be prepared in advance and reheated while cooking the prawns.

Variation
If using cooked prawns, reheat for about 5 minutes. Do not overcook.

SERVES 4

PLAICE WITH SPICY TOMATO SAUCE

This piquant fish dish is popular along
Mexico's Gulf coast.

90g/3oz cream cheese
5ml/1 tsp dried oregano
Pinch cayenne pepper
4 whole fillets of plaice
Lime slices and dill to garnish

Tomato Sauce

15ml/1 tbsp oil
1 small onion, chopped
1 stick celery, chopped
1 chilli pepper, seeded and chopped
1.25ml/¼ tsp each ground cumin, coriander and ginger
½ red and ½ green pepper, seeded and chopped
400g/14oz canned tomatoes
15ml/1 tbsp tomato purée
Salt, pepper and a pinch sugar

---

1. Heat the oil in a heavy-based pan and cook the onion, celery, chilli pepper and spices for about 5 minutes over very low heat.

2. Add red and green peppers and the remaining ingredients and bring to the boil. Reduce heat and simmer 15-20 minutes, stirring occasionally. Set aside while preparing the fish.

3. Mix the cream cheese, oregano and cayenne pepper together and set aside.

4. Skin the fillets using a filleting knife. Start at the tail end and hold the knife at a slight angle to the skin.

5. Push the knife along using a sawing motion, with the blade against the skin. Dip fingers in salt to make it easier to hold onto the fish skin. Gradually separate the fish from the skin.

6. Spread the cheese filling on all 4 fillets and roll each up. Secure with cocktail sticks.

7. Place the fillets in a lightly greased baking dish, cover and cook for 10 minutes in a preheated 180°C/350°F/Gas Mark 4 oven.

8. Pour over the tomato sauce and cook a further 10-15 minutes. Fish is cooked when it feels firm and looks opaque. Garnish with lime slices and dill.

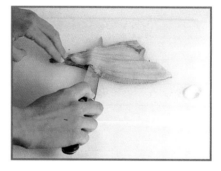

Step 5 Using a filleting knife held at an angle, push the knife along, cutting against the fish skin. Use a sawing motion to separate flesh from skin.

Step 6 Spread cheese filling on the fish and roll up each fillet.

Cook's Notes

Time
Preparation takes about 30 minutes and cooking takes 20-25 minutes.

Serving Ideas
Add rice and an avocado salad.

Special Occasions
Add prawns or crabmeat to the filling for a dinner party dish.

MAKES 6

EMPANADAS (SAVOURY TURNOVERS)

Fillings for these turnovers can also be sweet.
They are Spanish in origin and widely popular.

Triple quantity pastry recipe from Chilli Prawn Quiche
1 egg

Filling

1 onion, chopped
1 clove garlic, finely chopped
1 small green pepper, seeded and chopped
15ml/1 tbsp oil
225g/8oz minced beef
5ml/1 tsp cocoa powder
15g/1 tbsp flour
2.5ml/½ tsp ground cumin
2.5ml/½ tsp paprika
2.5ml/½ tsp dried oregano, crushed
Salt and pepper
1-2 chillies, seeded and chopped
30ml/2 tbsps tomato purée
45ml/3 tbsps water
30g/2 tbsps flaked almonds
30g/2 tbsps raisins

1. Prepare the pastry according to the recipe for Chilli Prawn Quiche, or use packaged shortcrust pastry.

2. Cook the onion, garlic and green pepper in the oil until soft but not coloured. Add the meat and fry quickly until well browned. Add the cocoa, flour, spices, oregano, and seasonings, stir well and cook briefly before adding the chillies, tomato purée and water. Cook slowly for 10-15 minutes. Add nuts and raisins and allow to cool.

3. Roll out the pastry on a floured surface and cut out 6 rounds using a 15cm/6 inch plate or saucepan lid as a guide.

4. Place the cooled filling on one side of the rounds of pastry and dampen the edges with water.

5. Fold over and press to seal the edges. Crimp the edges if desired.

6. Place on baking sheets and brush with a mixture of beaten egg and salt. Make sure the egg glaze is brushed on evenly. Prick once or twice with a fork and bake at 220°C/425°F/Gas Mark 7 for about 15 minutes, or until golden brown.

Step 5 Fold over and press the edges to seal firmly. Crimp if desired.

Step 6 Brush the surface of each turnover with beaten egg and prick the tops with a fork to let out steam.

Cook's Notes

Time
Preparation takes about 30 minutes. Dough should chill for about 30 minutes before rolling out. Filling takes about 20 minutes to cook and turnovers take about 15 minutes to bake.

Preparation
Turnovers may be baked in advance and reheated for about 5 minutes in a hot oven before serving. They may also be served cold.

Serving Ideas
Serve hot or cold as a snack or light meal accompanied with a salad. Perfect for picnics.

SERVES 4

Chilli con Carne

Although this dish is Mexican in
origin, the version everyone knows
best is really more American.

15ml/1 tbsp oil
450g/1lb minced beef
10ml/2 tsps ground cumin
10ml/2 tsps mild or hot chilli powder
Pinch oregano
Salt, pepper and pinch sugar
1.25ml/¼ tsp garlic granules
30ml/2 tbsps flour
450g/1lb canned tomatoes
450g/1lb canned red kidney beans

1. Heat the oil in a large saucepan and brown the meat, breaking it up with a fork as it cooks. Sprinkle on the cumin, chilli powder, oregano, salt, pepper, sugar, garlic and flour. Cook, stirring frequently, over medium heat for about 3 minutes.

2. Add the tomatoes and their liquid and simmer 25-30 minutes.

3. Drain the kidney beans and add just before serving. Heat through about 5 minutes.

Step 1 Sprinkle on the spice mixture and stir it into the meat. Skim off any fat that forms on the surface.

Step 2 Add the tomatoes and their liquid. Use a large spoon or potato masher to break up the tomatoes.

Cook's Notes

Time
Preparation takes about 15 minutes. Cooking takes about 10 minutes to brown the meat and 15-30 minutes to cook after the tomatoes are added.

Serving Ideas
Spoon the chilli on top of boiled rice to serve. Top with sour cream, chopped onion, grated cheese, diced avocado or a combination of the four ingredients.

Freezing
Allow the chilli to cool completely and place in rigid containers, seal, label and freeze for up to 3 months. Thaw before reheating.

SERVES 4

MEXICAN BEEF PATTIES

Refried beans added to the meat mixture
make moist and flavoursome beefburgers
that are slightly out of the ordinary.

1 onion, finely chopped
15ml/1 tbsp oil
340g/12oz minced beef
225g/8oz canned refried beans
60g/4 tbsps breadcrumbs
2.5ml/½ tsp cumin
5ml/1 tsp chilli powder
1 clove garlic, crushed
Salt and pepper
1 egg, beaten
Flour to coat
Oil for frying
Watercress to garnish

1. Cook the onion in the oil until soft but not browned. Mix in the beef, beans, breadcrumbs, spices, garlic and seasoning and gradually add the egg until the mixture holds together well.

2. Turn the mixture out onto a well-floured surface and divide into 8 pieces.

3. Shape into even-sized patties with well-floured hands. Knead the pieces before shaping, if necessary, to make sure mixture holds together with no cracks.

4. Coat lightly with flour and refrigerate until firm.

5. Pour enough oil into a large frying pan to completely cover the patties. Fry 2 at a time until golden brown on all sides and completely cooked through.

6. Remove from the oil and drain on paper towels. Arrange on a serving plate and garnish with watercress.

Step 3 Shape meat mixture into firm, even-sized patties with well-floured hands.

Step 4 Coat lightly with flour on all sides and place on a plate or baking sheet to refrigerate until firm.

Step 5 Fry 2 patties at a time in hot oil. Make sure they are completely submerged.

Cook's Notes

Time
Preparation takes about 20 minutes. The patties will take at least 1 hour to firm up sufficiently in the refrigerator.

Preparation
If mixture is too soft to shape, add 30g/2 tbsps flour.

Serving Ideas
Serve with sour cream or taco sauce and an avocado and tomato salad. Accompany with warm flour tortillas.

Freezing
Meat patties can be made up ahead of time and frozen on baking sheets until firm. Place in rigid containers with non-stick paper or wax paper between each patty. Defrost in the refrigerator before cooking. Do not use minced beef that has been previously frozen or defrosted.

SERVES 4

ALBONDIGAS (MEATBALLS)

A simple-to-make taco sauce makes plain meatballs
a lot less ordinary and a lot more fun to eat.

225g/8oz minced veal
225g/8oz minced beef
1 clove garlic, crushed
30g/2 tbsps dry breadcrumbs
½ chilli pepper, seeded and finely chopped
2.5ml/½ tsp ground cumin
Salt and pepper
1 egg, beaten
Oil for frying
Full quantity Taco Sauce recipe
2 spring onions, chopped

1. Mix together the veal, beef, garlic, breadcrumbs, chilli pepper, cumin, salt and egg until well blended. Add the egg gradually.

2. Turn the mixture out onto a floured surface and divide into 16 equal pieces.

3. With floured hands, shape the mixture into balls.

4. Pour about 45ml/3 tbsps of oil into a large frying pan and place over high heat.

5. When the oil is hot, place in the meatballs and fry for 5-10 minutes until brown on all sides. Turn frequently during cooking.

6. Remove the browned meatballs and drain well on paper towels. Place in an ovenproof dish and pour over the taco sauce.

7. Heat through in a preheated 170°C/350°F/Gas Mark 3 oven for 10 minutes. Sprinkle with chopped onions to serve.

Step 2 Divide the meat mixture into 16 equal pieces. Work on a floured surface.

Step 3 Flour hands well and roll each piece into a ball.

Step 5 Brown the meatballs on all sides in hot oil until a good colour.

Cook's Notes

Time
Preparation takes about 25 minutes and cooking time about 20 minutes.

Serving Ideas
Serve with rice, refried beans or guacamole. Drizzle with sour cream if desired.

Freezing
Prepare and cook the meatballs and allow to cool completely. Place meatballs on baking sheets and place in the freezer until firm. Transfer to freezer containers, label and store for up to 3 months. Defrost in the refrigerator and reheat according to the recipe.

SERVES 4

MEXICAN KEBABS

Kebabs are a favourite barbecue food
almost everywhere. The spice mixture and
sauce give these their Mexican flavour.

450g/1lb pork or lamb, cut into 5cm/2 inch pieces
120g/4oz large button mushrooms, left whole
2 medium onions, quartered
8 bay leaves
5ml/1 tsp cocoa powder
10ml/2 tsps chilli powder
1.25ml/¼ tsp garlic powder
2.5ml/½ tsp dried marjoram
Salt and pepper
90ml/6 tbsps oil
180g/6oz cooked rice
½ quantity Taco Sauce recipe

Step 3 Thread the meat and mushrooms onto skewers, alternating with onions and bay leaves.

Step 1 Place meat and mushrooms in a deep bowl with the marinade ingredients and stir to coat thoroughly.

Step 4 Place the kebabs on a lightly oiled rack and grill until meat is tender and onions are cooked. Baste frequently, using a small brush.

1. Place meat and mushrooms in a bowl. Add the bay leaves, cocoa, chilli powder, garlic powder, marjoram and seasoning to the oil and stir to coat all the ingredients with the marinade.

2. Cover the bowl and leave to marinate at least 6 hours, preferably overnight.

3. Remove meat, mushrooms and bay leaves from the marinade and reserve it. Thread onto skewers, alternating meat, onions, mushrooms and bay leaves.

4. Place under a preheated grill for 15-20 minutes, turning frequently until cooked to desired doneness. If using pork, the meat must be thoroughly cooked and not served pink. Baste with reserved marinade.

5. Mix hot rice with taco sauce and spoon onto a warm serving dish. Place the kebabs on top of the rice to serve.

Cook's Notes

Time
Preparation takes about 15 minutes, with at least 6 hours to marinate meat and mushrooms. Cooking time for the rice is about 12 minutes and 15-20 minutes for the meat.

Preparation
The kebabs may be cooked on an outdoor barbecue grill, if desired.

Variation
Add pieces of red or green pepper, cherry tomatoes or sliced courgettes to the kebabs and cut meat into slightly smaller pieces so everything cooks in the same length of time.

SERVES 4

SPARE RIBS IN CHILLI & CREAM SAUCE

Unsweetened cocoa lends colour and depth to a sauce for ribs that's slightly more sophisticated than the usual barbecue sauce.

1kg/2¼lbs spare ribs
5ml/1 tsp cocoa powder
15g/1 tbsp flour
2.5ml/½ tsp cumin
2.5ml/½ tsp paprika
2.5ml/½ tsp dried oregano, crushed
Salt and pepper
280ml/½ pint warm water
30ml/2 tbsps thin honey
30ml/2 tbsps double cream
Lime wedges and watercress for garnish

Step 2 Cook the ribs until the meat is tender to the point of a knife and the sauce is reduced.

Step 1 Cook the ribs until well browned. Remove from the roasting pan and pour off the fat.

Step 3 Place ribs on a chopping board and cut into pieces.

1. Leave the ribs in whole slabs and roast at 200°C/400°F/Gas Mark 6 for 20-25 minutes, or until well browned. Drain off all the excess fat.

2. Blend together the cocoa, flour, cumin, paprika, oregano, seasoning, water and honey and pour over the ribs. Lower the temperature to 180°C/350°F/Gas Mark 4

and cook ribs for a further 30 minutes, until the sauce has reduced and the ribs are tender.

3. Cut the ribs into pieces and arrange on a serving dish.

4. Pour the cream into the sauce in the roasting pan and place over moderate heat. Bring to the boil and pour over the ribs.

5. Garnish with lime wedges and serve.

Cook's Notes

Time
Preparation takes about 20 minutes, cooking takes 50-55 minutes.

Preparation
Ribs may be cooked for the last 30 minutes on an outdoor barbecue grill.

Serving Ideas
Serve with rice and an avocado or tomato salad.

SERVES 6

MINUTE STEAKS WITH TACO SAUCE

A quick meal needn't be ordinary. Prepare taco sauce ahead
and keep it on hand to add last-minute spice to a meal.

Full quantity Taco Sauce recipe
30g/1oz butter or margarine
30ml/2 tbsps oil
6 minute steaks
Salt and pepper
120g/4oz button mushrooms, left whole
Chopped parsley or coriander leaves

1. Prepare taco sauce according to the recipe directions.
Heat the butter or margarine and oil together in a large
frying or sauté pan. Season the steaks with salt and pepper
and fry 2 or 3 at a time for 2-3 minutes on each side, or to
desired doneness.

2. Remove the steaks to a warm serving dish and add the
mushrooms to the pan. Sauté over high heat to brown
lightly, remove and keep warm.

3. Drain most of the fat from the pan and pour in the taco
sauce. Place over low heat until just bubbling. Spoon over
the steaks.

4. Top the steaks with the sautéed mushrooms and
sprinkle over parsley or coriander before serving.

Step 1 Cook
steaks over high
heat until done to
desired degree.
To check, make a
small cut in the
centre.

Step 2 Add
mushrooms to the
pan and cook
briskly until lightly
browned.

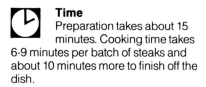

 Time
Preparation takes about 15
minutes. Cooking time takes
6-9 minutes per batch of steaks and
about 10 minutes more to finish off the
dish.

Variation
Substitute turkey escalopes
for the steaks, if desired, and
cook until juices run clear.

 Serving Ideas
Serve with rice or flour tortillas.

SERVES 4

LEG OF LAMB WITH CHILLI SAUCE

Give Sunday roast lamb a completely
different taste with a spicy orange sauce.

1kg/2¼lb leg of lamb

Marinade

5ml/1 tsp cocoa powder
1.25ml/¼ tsp cayenne pepper
2.5ml/½ tsp ground cumin
2.5ml/½ tsp paprika
2.5ml/½ tsp ground oregano
140ml/¼ pint water
140ml/¼ pint orange juice
140ml/¼ pint red wine
1 clove of garlic, crushed
30g/2 tbsps brown sugar
15ml/1 tbsp cornflour
Pinch salt
Orange slices and coriander to garnish

1. If the lamb has a lot of surface fat, trim slightly with a sharp knife. If possible, remove the paper-thin skin on the outside of the lamb. Place lamb in a shallow dish.

2. Mix together the marinade ingredients, except cornflour, and pour over the lamb, turning it well to coat completely. Cover and refrigerate for 12-24 hours, turning occasionally.

3. Drain the lamb, reserving the marinade, and place in a roasting pan. Cook in a preheated 180°C/350°F/Gas Mark 4 oven for about 2 hours until meat is cooked according to taste.

4. Baste occasionally with the marinade and pan juices.

5. Remove lamb to a serving dish and keep warm. Skim the fat from the top of the roasting pan with a large spoon and discard.

6. Pour remaining marinade into the pan juices in the roasting pan and bring to the boil, stirring to loosen the sediment. Mix cornflour with a small amount of water and add some of the liquid from the roasting pan. Gradually stir cornflour mixture into the pan and bring back to the boil.

7. Cook, stirring constantly, until thickened and clear. Add more orange juice, wine or water as necessary.

8. Garnish the lamb with orange slices and sprigs of coriander. Pour over some of the sauce and serve the rest separately.

Step 6 Pour the marinade into the roasting pan and bring to the boil. Scrape to remove browned juices.

Step 7 Cook, stirring constantly, until thickened and clear. Add more orange juice, wine or water as necessary.

Cook's Notes

Time
Preparation takes about 15 minutes, with 12-24 hours for the lamb to marinate. Cooking takes about 2 hours for the lamb and 20 minutes to finish the sauce.

Cook's Tip
The marinade ingredients can also be used with beef or poultry.

Serving Ideas
Serve with rice or boiled potatoes and vegetables.

SERVES 6

MANGO FOOL

To cool the palate after a spicy
Mexican meal, the taste of mango,
lime, ginger and cream is perfect.

2 ripe mangoes
1 small piece fresh ginger, peeled and shredded
120g/4oz sifted icing sugar
Juice of ½ a lime
280ml/½ pint double cream

Step 3 Whisk the cream to soft peaks.

Step 1 Cut the mango in half, slicing around the stone. Scoop out pulp.

Step 3 Fold the cream into the mango purée using a large spoon or rubber spatula.

1. Cut the mangoes in half, cutting around the stone. Scoop out the pulp into a bowl, blender or food processor. Reserve two slices.

2. Add the ginger, icing sugar and lime juice and purée in the blender or food processor until smooth. Use a hand blender or electric mixer in the bowl, pushing mixture through a sieve afterwards, if necessary.

3. Whip the cream until soft peaks form and fold into the

mango purée.

4. Divide the mixture between 6 glass serving dishes and leave in the refrigerator for 1 hour before serving.

5. Cut the reserved mango slices into 6 smaller slices or pieces and garnish the fool.

Cook's Notes

 Time
Preparation takes about 20 minutes. Fool should be refrigerated 1 hour before serving.

Serving Ideas
Accompany with biscuits.

Watchpoint
When whipping cream, refrigerate it for at least 2 hours before use. Overwhisked cream turns to butter, so whisk slowly and watch carefully.

SERVES 6

TROPICAL FRUIT SALAD

A refreshing mixture of exotic fruits is the
most popular sweet in Mexico. Add tequila or
triple sec to the syrup for a special occasion.

½ cantaloup or honeydew melon, cubed or made into
   balls
½ small fresh pineapple, peeled, cored and cubed or
   sliced
120g/4oz fresh strawberries, hulled and halved (leave
   whole, if small)
1 mango, peeled and sliced or cubed
225g/8oz watermelon, seeded and cubed
120g/4oz guava or papaya, peeled and cubed
2 oranges, peeled and segmented
1 prickly pear, peeled and sliced (optional)
120g/4oz sugar
140ml/¼ pint water
Grated rind and juice of 1 lemon
30g/2 tbsps chopped pecans to garnish (optional)

1. To make melon balls, cut melons in half and scoop out
seeds and discard them. To use a melon baller, press
cutting edge firmly into the melon flesh and twist around to
scoop out round pieces.

2. It is easy to core the pineapple if it is first cut into quarters.
Use a serrated fruit knife to cut the point off the quarter,
removing the core. Slice off the peel. Cut into slices or cubes
and mix with the other fruit.

3. Dissolve the sugar in the water over gentle heat and
when the mixture is no longer grainy, leave it to cool
completely.

4. Add lemon rind and juice to the sugar syrup and pour
over the prepared fruit. Refrigerate well before serving.
Sprinkle with chopped nuts, if desired.

Step 1 Cut melon in half and scoop out seeds.

Step 1 Twist melon baller around to scoop out round shaped pieces.

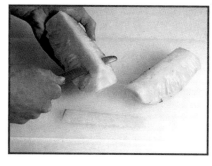

Step 2 Cut out pineapple core with a serrated fruit knife.

Cook's Notes

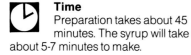

Time
Preparation takes about 45
minutes. The syrup will take
about 5-7 minutes to make.

Preparation
Allow the syrup to cool
completely before adding any
fruit. Hot syrup will cook the fruit and
draw out the juices.

Variation
Use other varieties of fruit,
choosing whatever is in
season.

SERVES 4

MEXICAN CHOCOLATE FLAN

Flan in Mexico is a moulded custard with
a caramel sauce. Chocolate and cinnamon
is a favourite flavour combination.

120g/4oz sugar
30ml/2 tbsps water
Juice of ½ a lemon
280ml/½ pint milk
60g/2oz plain chocolate
1 cinnamon stick
2 whole eggs
2 egg yolks
60g/4 tbsps sugar

1. Combine the first amount of sugar with the water and lemon juice in a small, heavy-based saucepan.

2. Cook over gentle heat until the sugar starts to dissolve. Swirl the pan from time to time, but don't stir.

3. Once the sugar liquifies, bring the syrup to the boil and cook until golden brown.

4. While preparing the syrup, heat 4 ramekin dishes in a 180°C/350°F/Gas Mark 4 oven. When the syrup is ready, pour into the dishes and swirl to coat the sides and base evenly. Leave to cool at room temperature.

5. Chop the chocolate into small pieces and heat with the milk and cinnamon, stirring occasionally to help chocolate dissolve.

6. Whisk the whole eggs and the yolks together with the remaining sugar until slightly frothy. Gradually whisk in the chocolate milk. Remove cinnamon.

7. Pour the chocolate custard carefully into the ramekin

dishes and place them in a roasting pan of hand-hot water.

8. Place the roasting pan in the oven and bake the custards until just slightly wobbly in the centre, about 20-30 minutes. Cool at room temperature and refrigerate for several hours or overnight before serving. Loosen custards carefully from the sides of the dishes and invert into serving plates. Shake to allow custard to drop out.

Step 3 Boil sugar syrup rapidly until golden brown.

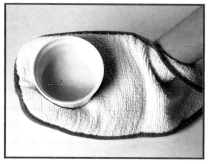

Step 4 Pour caramel into warmed dishes and swirl to coat base and sides.

 Cook's Notes

 Time
Preparation takes about 30 minutes, cooking takes about 35-40 minutes.

 Variation
Leave out chocolate, if desired, for cinnamon flan.

 Watchpoint
Do not allow custard to over-cook or it will form a tough skin on top. If the oven temperature is too high, it will cause the custard to boil and spoil the texture.

 Serving Ideas
Garnish with pecans or chocolate curls. Also good with fruit such as raspberries or bananas with chocolate; peaches or strawberries with cinnamon.

SERVES 4

TEQUILA SUNRISE

120ml/4 fl oz tequila
430ml/¾ pint orange juice
60ml/4 tbsp Cointreau or Grand Marnier
Ice
60ml/4 tbsps Grenadine syrup

1. Crush ice and place in a blender with the tequila, orange juice and orange liqueur and mix thoroughly.

2. Chill 4 tall glasses in the refrigerator and when cold, pour in the cocktail mixture.

3. Hold each glass at a tilt and carefully pour 15ml/1 tbsp

Hold glass at a tilt and carefully pour grenadine down the side for the tequila sunrise.

Grenadine syrup down one side. Syrup will sink to the bottom giving the drink its sunrise effect.

SERVES 2

MARGARITA

1 lime
Coarse salt
120ml/4 fl oz tequila
30ml/2 tbsps triple sec
4 ice cubes

1. Squeeze the lime and moisten the rim of two cocktail

glasses with a small amount of juice.

2. Pour salt onto a plate and dip in the moistened rims of the glasses, turning to coat evenly. Refrigerate to chill thoroughly.

3. Crush 4 ice cubes and place in a blender with the tequila and triple sec. Process until well blended and slushy. Pour into the chilled glasses and serve immediately.

Rub rims of cocktail glasses with half a lime to moisten for the margarita.

Pour salt onto a plate and dip in the moistened rims of the glasses.

INDEX

Compiled by Judith Ferguson
Photographed by Peter Barry
Recipes Prepared for Photography by
Jacqueline Bellefontaine

Acknowledgement
The publishers wish to thank Old El Paso for permission to feature
their recipes for Leg of Lamb with Chilli Sauce, Spare Ribs in
Chilli and Cream Sauce, Mexican Kebabs, Mexican Beef Patties,
and Minute Steaks with Taco Sauce